TO

FROM

DATE

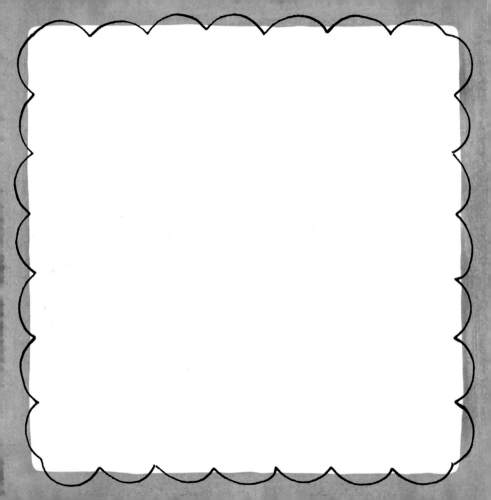

GIRLFRIEND CONNECTIONS

Moments of Adventure

GIRLFRIEND CONNECTIONS

Moments of Adventure

by Bonnie Jensen

BARBOUR
PUBLISHING

Illustrated by Julie Sawyer. Designed by Greg Jackson.

Published by Barbour Publishing, Inc., P.O. Box 719, Uhrichsville, Ohio 44683
www.barbourbooks.com

Our mission is to publish and distribute inspirational products offering exceptional value and biblical encouragement to the masses.

Member of the
Evangelical Christian
Publishers Association

Printed in China.
5 4 3 2 1

Adventure. . .

Shopping sprees. Cooking classes. Chick flicks.
Scrapbooking. Girlfriends embark on joint
ventures because they know how important it is
to infuse their relationships with laughter and
shared experiences. They build memories while
nurturing a deep appreciation for their friendship.
This little book explores the endeavors girlfriends
enjoy—together—and the "heart-connections"
that are strengthened through these delightful,
unforgettable adventures.

We are brave in the face

of new experiences

if we have a faithful friend

to journey with us.

The courage to try different things

is one part curiosity and two parts

the inspiration of a friend.

True friendship isn't measured by time,
but by the times shared.

KELLY EILEEN HAKE

Girlfriends are true

sources of inspiration.

There are two things one should

know about the direction of life.

First is: Where am I going?

Second is: Who will go with me?

ELIE WIESEL

Hand-in-hand with a friend

our hearts are bolder. . .

and we're willing to stretch

our faith a little further.

The courtesy of taking

turns never grows old—

It's my turn to choose the movie. . . .

It's your turn to choose the restaurant. . . .

It's my turn to choose the dessert. . . .

Girlfriends will take you on more
adventures than you can count.

$\mathcal{M}$y girlfriends and I dreamed of having

a playhouse and all the dolls we wanted. . .a car of

our own to take us anywhere we wanted to go. . .

a job we loved, a husband, a family. . .and suddenly

we realized—our dreams grew up as fast as we did.

$\mathcal{O}$ur girlfriends have a way of bringing out the adventurer in us (even when we'd rather be hiding out at home).

K. WILLIAMS

Girlfriends just know how
to have fun—TOGETHER!

$\mathcal{L}$ife is a chronicle of friendship.

Friends create the world anew each day.

Without their loving care, courage would

not suffice to keep hearts strong for life.

HELEN KELLER

I wouldn't trade my girlfriends for anything in the world! They renew my sense of adventure by opening my eyes to the joy of discovering things I would never see for myself.

God meant for us to have friends.

It's His way of helping us see the world

through different eyes than our own.

When you're safe at home you wish

you were having an adventure. . . .

THORNTON WILDER

How many adventures
have been the result
of a friend saying,
"I dare you!"
or "PLEEEASE"?

Girlfriends have a special way of turning the ordinary and mundane into extraordinary and fun.

K. WILLIAMS

When a shopping trip with girlfriends is planned
for the day, it's amazing how that internal alarm
screams to awaken you bright and early
(when otherwise it would lie dormant).

Men just don't understand
shopping like women do.
Men liken the experience
to a spending spree, but it's
really more like an opportunity
to channel creative energy.

ANITA WIEGAND

ADVENTURES in SHOPPING

The Top Five Reasons to Buy That Handbag

5. It comes with compartments to store all the essentials—cell phone, lip gloss, charge card. . .

4. There's no way this one will make it to the sales table.

3. Women are all about a handbag for every occasion, and that new car wash opens tomorrow.

2. Pink goes with everything, doesn't it?

1. Well, maybe there aren't five good reasons, but the other four are reason enough!

Some days it's adventure enough to
try the flavor of the month at the local
ice cream parlor—and more fun, of course,
if you're with a friend who appreciates
the outing as much as you do!

Having a variety of experiences

with our girlfriends can help

open our hearts and minds

and enable us to appreciate

the diversity God created.

God has given us these times of joy.

PSALM 81:4 TLB

Planning a weekend getaway with girlfriends
is a little about escaping the day-to-day
routine of our hectic lives and a lot about
spending precious, uninterrupted
time with our friends.

Enjoy the little things, for one day
you may look back and discover
they were the big things.

UNKNOWN

Anticipating and planning an

adventure with our girlfriends

is almost as much fun as going

on one—even if it doesn't happen,

we have a great time talking about it!

A day is simply a collection of moments;

it is our friends who make them happy ones.

$\mathcal{A}$ true friend unbosoms freely,

advises justly, assists readily, adventures boldly,

takes all patiently, defends courageously,

and continues a friend unchangeably.

WILLIAM PENN

*a*dventures with girlfriends. . .
Love, laughter, and conversation

are the main ingredients!

Good times are made even better
when they're shared with a friend.

Getting together with our girlfriends
means two things—comfortable shoes
(for shopping) and comfortable
waistbands (for having dessert).

We shouldn't allow too much
time to lapse between having adventures
with our girlfriends—laughter
and silliness are good for the soul.

It's important to make time to do "girl things"—

like shopping trips, afternoon matinees

(to view movies the guys will never see), and stops

at restaurants best known for their tasty desserts.

Those who bring sunshine to the lives
of others cannot keep it from themselves.

SIR JAMES MATTHEW BARRIE

Having a circle of unique girlfriends
is like having a wealth of experience and
adventure you can tap into at any given time.

Good company through life's
journey makes the adventure
seem more exciting and
the road easier to travel.

I thank the Lord for
my traveling companions!

We can be ourselves

around our girlfriends.

(It is one of life's greatest pleasures.)

*I*s there anything so enjoyable

as a warm cup of coffee, laughter,

a good conversation, and a great friend?

Girlfriends can act silly, forgo makeup,

wear whatever they feel like wearing,

and never worry about being

accepted for who they are.

Going different places and doing new
things is only half the fun. . . .
Sharing the experience with a friend
fills the time with joy.

Each of our friends brings something wonderful into our lives. It is our gift to them to encourage their uniqueness, affirm their strengths, and appreciate the happiness they add to our days.

We all need at least one spontaneous friend. . . .

She'll open the door to adventures

we would never take on our own!

As friends, we do things together
to build memories;
they're the keepsakes that become
a source of joy when we're apart.

ADVENTURES in SHOPPING

Four Good Reasons to Buy Another Pair of Shoes

4. The sale racks are overcrowded.

3. You need one more pair to balance
   your shoe rack at home.

2. It might be a good idea to keep a spare pair in the
   car—just in case you feel the need to change styles.

1. You have some extra time—and an hour
   in the shoe department is time well spent.

Going to aerobics class is reminiscent of taking trips to the girls' room in high school—it feels better when two or three of your girlfriends go with you.

$\mathcal{G}$irlfriends need to spend time

together for lots of reasons. . .

and sometimes for no reason at all.

Good friendships are home-like—
welcoming, sheltering, and comfortable.

*F*riendships must be nurtured,

enjoyed, protected—and time is an

essential part of caring for them.

When lack of time prevents us from
doing things with our friends,
perhaps we'll be given the perfect
opportunity to do something FOR them.

Adventure encompasses not only the fun times we spend with our girlfriends. . .but also the times we make those heart-connections with them over coffee or dessert.

$\mathcal{T}$rue friends are those who
are better together than either
of them could be alone.

ANONYMOUS

Oftentimes it is our friends who
encourage us to venture beyond the
places we've already been—to try
the things we never thought possible.

See, I am doing a new thing!

Now it springs up;

do you not perceive it?

ISAIAH 43:19

When I go places with my friends,

the drive to where we're going

is as much fun as getting there!

Good company upon the
road is the shortest cut.

ANONYMOUS

It is a great gift from God to go through life with a small number of really good friends to call your very own.

Only women understand
that shopping with a friend
is efficient; it doubles
our chances of finding exactly
what we're looking for.

What a thing friendship is,

world without end!

How it gives the heart

and soul a stir-up!

ROBERT BROWNING

*I*nto all lives, in many simple, familiar, homely ways, God infuses this element of joy from the surprises of life, which unexpectedly brighten our days, and fill our eyes with light.

HENRY WADSWORTH LONGFELLOW

Because of our routines we often forget that life is an ongoing adventure.

MAYA ANGELOU

There's no such thing as too many girlfriends!
The chance to make a new friend is like being
offered dessert—you can always make room!

$\mathcal{K}$eep on loving your friends;
do your work in welcoming hearts.

PSALM 36:10 MSG

You know you've made a new friend when. . .

You find yourselves laughing at the same jokes.

You discover you like the same books and movies.

You find yourselves talking faster and faster,

trying to find out everything about each other.

The differences you find only make the other

person seem more interesting.

ELLYN SANNA

God has paved our journey
through the adventure of life. . . .
Our friends are the flowers
He planted along the way.

Friendship is unnecessary, like philosophy, like art. . . . It has no survival value; rather is one of those things that gives value to survival.

C. S. LEWIS

The relationship between girlfriends is about give and take. At times we give more than we take and at other times we rely heavily on our friendships—but in a true friendship it all evens out in the end.

ANITA WIEGAND

$\mathcal{A}$ real friend helps us think
our best thoughts, do our noblest
deeds, be our finest selves.

ANONYMOUS

If you have but one true,

faithful friend,

you'll have adventures

without end.

Dreams are adventures you invite

only your closest friends to share. . .

for they are the ones who will give you

the courage and the wings to reach them.

Life itself is a quest—one that requires

the company and comfort of friends.

Some days you just gotta go all out

and try that wild new nail polish.

(It's much safer while getting

a manicure with a girlfriend.)

I had three chairs in my house:

one for solitude, two for friendship. . . .

HENRY DAVID THOREAU

Each new day may uncover something
wonderful or something difficult.
The blessing of having friends is the
assurance that we can rely on them
no matter what the day brings.

To be glad of life because it gives you the chance to love and to work and to play and to look up at the stars. . .to think. . .often of your friends, and every day of Christ. . .these are little guideposts on the footpath of peace.

HENRY VAN DYKE

The company makes the feast.

ANONYMOUS

Girlfriends are good for walking

beside you. . .and going ahead of you

when you need someone to show the way.

May the Lord continually bless
you with heaven's blessings
as well as with human joys.

PSALM 128:5 TLB

$\mathcal{A}$n occasional girls' night out

is a mandatory part of

maintaining your sanity.

There are endless demands on our time—
maybe that's what makes the time we spend
with our girlfriends feel like such a luxury.

Girlfriends who shop together develop a certain rhythm; it's sort of a timing mechanism that sends a signal from one to the other when they're ready to move from one store to the next.

Is it so small a thing
To have enjoyed the sun,
To have lived light in the spring,
To have loved, to have thought, to have done;
To have advanced true friends. . . .

M. ARNOLD

There's no other adventure as wonderful as having a group of girlfriends to talk, walk, dine, shop, cry, laugh, travel, or simply enjoy life with—they're one of the greatest sources of happiness God put in our world.

Memory has painted this perfect day
With colors that never fade,
And we find at the end of a perfect day
The soul of a friend we've made.

C. J. BONDS

Where there is trust, comfort, and laughter, there is friendship worth cherishing with your whole heart.

God, who got you started in

this spiritual adventure. . .

will never give up on you.

Never forget that.

1 CORINTHIANS 1:9 MSG

Shopping sprees...cooking classes...
chick flicks...scrapbooking...

Embark on an "adventure" with
your girlfriends and embrace the pleasures
of the exhilarating spirit of friendship.

Illustrated by
Julie Sawyer

$7.95 U.S.
ISBN 1-59310-621-1

EAN

9 781593 106218

INSPIRATIONAL / GIFT BOOKS / GENERAL

09-BRV-887